John Jessie Bruce

A Trip to Florida, Spring of 1883

John Jessie Bruce

A Trip to Florida, Spring of 1883

ISBN/EAN: 9783337144470

Printed in Europe, USA, Canada, Australia, Japan

Cover: Foto ©Andreas Hilbeck / pixelio.de

More available books at **www.hansebooks.com**

A TRIP TO FLORIDA,

SPRING OF 1883.

By JOHN JESSIE BRUCE.

CUMBERLAND, MD.
THE DAILY NEWS.
1883.

A Trip to Florida.

Tuesday, April 3, 1883. —This morning dawned a glorious bright day, and was hailed with delight by three very impatient persons, who were all excitement to leave the " Forest City " for the " Land of Flowers." These three were Mrs. George A. Mercer, of Savannah ; Miss Hattie Cope, of Savannah ; Miss John Jessie Bruce, of Cumberland, Maryland. The latter (the writer) was on a visit to Mrs. Mercer, and she was going to take Hattie and me to Florida to spend a week. We were to leave on the steamer " City of Bridgeton " at four o'clock in the afternoon ; so punctually at that hour we were on deck, waiting impatiently for the bell to ring. After waiting until half-past four, the Captain told us that the steamer would not leave until ten o'clock that night.

So we left the boat, and Mrs. Mercer went up to her house, promising to meet us at Hamilton's store at six o'clock. Hattie, Mr. Botts (a brother-in-law of Mrs. Mercer) and I roamed around the streets, bought candy, pickles, crackers and cheese. At six o'clock we were at Hamilton's, but Mrs. Mercer did not come until nearly seven. So we three, with Mr. Botts, Capt. Mercer, Mr. Robert Mercer and George, wended our way down to the wharf, and once again left terra firma and stepped on the steamer, there to remain until we reached Fernandina We had tea composed of our evening's purchases. As the boat moved off, Hattie and I stood on deck, and sang our favorite song, "Jaunita." After leaving Savannah in the dim distance, we sat in the saloon and read for an hour. Then we thought of bed. Mrs. Mercer had her stateroom just opposite ours, Hattie and I having one together. In a short time our tired heads were on our pillows, and before very long we were all in the "Land of Nod." At one o'clock we awoke and thought certainly every moment would be our last. We decided to go to Mrs. Mercer and see if she could tell us what was the matter. She laughed at us, and told us that we were going through St. Catharine's Sound, and had grounded. Of course we were very much relieved, and went back to our own rooms, there to lean out of the window until nearly morning, eating pickles, cheese and candy.

The first sound we heard in the morning was the breakfast bell, and we all hurried down to come back with that delightful meal untouched. Such a breakfast! We sat on deck, and read aloud until dinner, which was at one o'clock. We did enjoy our dinner, and came up on deck to watch the boat nearing Fernandina, until we touched its shores. The water was filled with sails, and seemed like a beautiful picture. After leaving the boat we immediately took a carriage to drive to the ocean. The celebrated Amelia Beach is one mile from Fernandina, and the road is shells. The drive is not particularly pretty, there being no trees, and only palms of a stunted growth on either side. Some half mile from town there is a light-house, and from there you get the first glimpse of the ocean. We reached the beach about half past four, nearly high tide. It would be impossible to describe the grandeur of the scene; it was awful! Far away, some ten or twelve miles, there was one solitary sail battling with the waves. After driving around the beach for half an hour we turned our backs on old ocean, and a few minutes' ride brought us again into Fernandina We went to the Egmont Hotel, which is one of the prettiest in Florida. It is kept by Northerners, so of course there is nothing lacking in the way of comfort. After resting there for a few minutes, we determined to " do " the town, but as Mrs. Mercer was too tired, we left her at the station in charge of the satchels, and Hattie and I walked around. The town is very old, but not very interesting, and the little there was to see we thoroughly enjoyed. About six o'clock we returned to Mrs. Mercer, and just as we had seated ourselves, the train for Jacksonville came snorting and puffing in. It did not wait long, and presently we were hurrying along farther south. The country is painfully flat, and the scenery from Fernandina to Jacksonville anything but pretty. At eight o'clock we reached our destination, took a tram-car and went directly to the Windsor Hotel. The house was full, but by some fortunate accident there was one room unoccupied, and in that one Mrs. Mercer, Hattie and I slept. We sat on the porch for a little while, but were so tired that we determined that bed was the best place for us.

Thursday morning was one of the warmest days I ever experienced. We got up about seven o'clock. Of course the first thing we did was to look out. We were delighted with the limited view obtained from a hotel window, and made numerous plans for the day. By nine o'clock we had finished breakfast, and started out to see the city. The Windsor

House is generally considered the finest hotel
in Jacksonville. Certainly it is beautifully
kept. Directly on the other side of the park
stands the St. James. There are three other
large hotels in the town, beside numerous
boarding-houses. One peculiarity of Florida
is, that it has no theaters of any kind. The
Episcopal church is a little beauty. The trees
in Jacksonville grow to an immense size, and
there are rows on each side of every street.
The streets are not paved, and with a few excep-
tions the sidewalks are made of planks. Of
course the liveliest, as well as the most interesting place is the "bay." Here most of the
stores are, and during the "Florida Season"
you might imagine from the number of people
you meet that you were in one of the Northern cities. We went into most of the curiosity
stores, and saw alligators, birds, flowers, and
every other animal and vegetable peculiar to
the extreme south. After wandering around
until half past one, we came back and sat on
the porch, listening to some little negro boys
singing darkey songs. At two o'clock we started for the boat to go up the St. Johns. After
waiting some time on the hot, dirty wharf,
the bell rang, and we boarded the handsomest
steamer on the river—the "City of Jacksonville" of the De Barry line. From Jacksonville
to Palatka the river is very broad, being from

two to six miles wide. At six o'clock we stopped at Magnolia for a few moments. Almost beside Magnolia is Green Cove Spring. It is a beautifnl little place. We passed and had a glimpse of " Mandarin " the well known winter home of the celebrated authoress of " Uncle Tom's Cabin," Harriet Beecher Stone. Just a little before reaching Palatka we pass Tocoi. Here the railroad runs to St Augustine, a distance of fifteen miles. At eight o'clock we reached Palatka, and Mrs Mercer, Hattie and I, under the chaperonage of the Captain, walked around the town. The hotels are very good, especially the Putnam House. At Palatka you take the steamer for the Ocklawaha river   The town is filled with taxidermists, the most noted one being Mr. J H. Fry. After looking around for about an hour we went back to our boat.   For some time we sat on deck, watching the lovely moon-lit waters. About eleven o'clock we went to our staterooms, Hattie and I together, and Mrs. Mercer next to us. Just before reaching Palatka we came to Lake George. It is considered the finest sheet of water in Florida, having a surface of one hundred square miles, being twelve miles long by nine wide. That night we all enjoyed a good rest.

Some time before Hattie was awake in the morning I was dressed, and watching the alligators and beautiful birds along the shore. We passed any quantity of pelicans, pink curlew, brown curlew, ducks and cranes. The river from De Land Landing to Lake Monroe is so narrow that you can reach out and touch the foliage on the banks. The scenery must be left to the imagination,for no pen can describe it. The trees are entirely different from the Northern trees. The palms are tall and stately, and everything has a tropical look. After having a most delightful breakfast, we went up on deck, and saw in the far distance Sanford on one side of Lake Monroe, and Enterprise on the other, the lake itself being five miles wide. We reached Enterprise about nine o'clock Friday morning, landed and went up to the hotel, the Block House. After looking around there a few moments we went over to an orange grove, and Hattie and I climbed the trees and ate oranges to our heart's content. The fruit in Florida is the most delicious one can imagine. After getting on the boat again we crossed over to Sanford, and looked around there for a little while. About eleven o'clock we boarded the " City of Jacksonville " again, and once more turned our faces toward Palatka. We sat on deck and read until dinner, and after dinner went into our state-rooms to take a nap The heat was almost unbearable. About six o'clock we came out, had our suppers, and watched the river until we reached Palatka, which was about half past seven. We went directly to the Putnam House, expecting to stay there until the next morning. On our arrival two telegrams were given to us from Capt Mercer, saying that President Arthur would pass through Palatka at eleven o'clock that night, on the steamer "De Barry," and that he wanted us to meet him. At first we thought we would not go, as we were very tired, but after due consideration we decided to go to our rooms and take a little nap before the boat came in. So we unpacked our valises (we had only one dress each with us) and arranged everything for the night, told the porter to call us at half past ten, and then laid down to doze for a little while. The night was almost unbearable on account of the heat, but we managed after eating a great deal of ice, and fanning vigorously, to sleep until a voice at the door calling "ten minutes until the boat arrives," wakened us from our much needed slumbers. We dressed in a terrible hurry and ran out on the porch to inquire if the boat had left. We found that it had not come, and so we determined to sit on the porch until we heard the whistle. Twelve o'clock came, and one, and still we had not left the Putnam. We waited patiently, eating delicious oranges, and doing our best to knock some sour ones from

trees in front of the hotel. About two o'clock
we heard the boat and started for the wharf.
When we reached there the "De Barry" was
in, and "Alick," the President's valet, called
out and asked if Mrs Mercer was there. When
he found that she was on the pier, he told her
that the President was asleep, but that he had
engaged state-rooms for us, and wanted us to
go up the river with him. Of course Hattie
and I were in extacies, but Mrs. Mercer thought
as we had been up the river there was no neces.
sity for our going again. However, we begged
and she consented; so with all haste imaginable
we three plodded back to the hotel, packed our
valises, and were on the steamer in fifteen
minutes from the time we had left. As it was
so late, Hattie and I did not see the President,
but Mrs. Mercer, being a near relative, had
quite a little talk with him. Before very long
we were all in the arms of Morpheus.

The following morning Hattie, Mrs. Mercer
and I went out on deck about nine o'clock and
there met Mr. Phillips, the President's private
secretary; Mr. Miller, a friend of President
Arthur's from New York; Secretary of the
Navy Chandler, and Reginald Fry of New
York. We went to breakfast about half past
nine. We had a separate table, and of course,
were the "observed of all observers" Breakfast being over, we went to the aft part of the

boat, and had a real jolly time until eleven
o'clock, when the President walked out upon
us Soon we found that he was bright, humor-
ous and fascinating. About one o'clock we
reached Enterprise, when a darkey came out
and presented the President with an eagle. Of
course he had no place to put it, so he kindly
and politely refused. Arriving at Sanford at
two, we went immediately to the Sanford
House, where our rooms were engaged. We
had one corridor on the second floor entirely
to ourselves. Outside of all of our windows
there was a beautiful wide piazza running the
entire length of the building, and there we
could sit and enjoy the delightful breeze from
Lake Monroe After having some lunch, we
got into buggies and drove to Belle View, a
large orange grove, owned by Mr. Sanford.
We there saw growing oranges, bananas, figs,
pine apples, tea, coffee, pepper, camphor,
lemons, Surnam cherries and numerous other
tropical fruits. We were followed by four
newspaper reporters. We drove home late
that evening, and found a delicious dinner
waiting for us. Just before going to the dining
room, I was surprised by some one coming up
to me and saying, "Is this Miss Jessie Bruce?"
He introduced himself, and of conrse I immediately recognized in him the most stupid man
that Cumberland ever sent forth. I excused

myself until after dinner, but before I was
seated in the hall he came and asked me to
talk to him. Of course I was obliged to do so
I never knew the minutes to go so slowly.
They seemed to have weights attached to them.
We sat there for some time, I wishing that I
was over with our party, and he thinking that
I was an intensely uninteresting damsel Being
Saturday night he left about half past eleven,
and no one knows with what joy I joined my
friends. Hattie and I had a room together,
and Mrs. Mercer's door opened into it. We
walked on the porch for some time after going
up stairs, and Hattie quite conquered the President. We slept very soundly that night, and
awoke about eight o'clock the following morning.

The night before Hattie saw an old servant
that she was quite fond of, so she came in and
talked to us for some time. Before we were
ready the next morning (Sunday) Mr. Miller
and Secretary Chandler were at our windows
begging us to come and walk before
breakfast. We had a nice little talk on the
porch before President Arthur and Mr. Phillips
were ready, consequently we had good appe-
tites for a nice breakfast. About eleven o'clock
President Arthur, Hattie, Mrs. Mercer, Secretary Chandler and I went to church. When
we reached home about one, we did ample jus-

tice to the lemonade and crackers which had been prepared for us. Hattie and I were very anxious to take a sulphur bath, so she and I, with Mrs. Mercer, started off in a partly covered wagon, with a little boy driving. On reaching the bath houses we immediately set to work to enjoy one of nature's own luxuries. Hattie tried to teach me to float, with a little success and a great deal of trouble. On our way home a terrific rain came up and I was wet through and through. Hattie and Mrs. Mercer were under cover and escaped with very little harm. When we reached our rooms I was in a peck of trouble, for we had brought only one change of clothing with us, and it was at the laundry. However I managed to have my clothes dried in the kitchen. When we went down to din- ner we had a good laugh. The gentlemen de- clared that we smelt so of sulphur that they could not have us near them. It certainly was a jolly party. After dinner we all walked on the piazza for a while, and then sat around and talked until bed-time, deciding to go down to Kissimee City in the morning.

Monday turned out to be a perfect day, and before anyone else was out, Mr. Miller and I were at the stores buying fish hooks. Eleven o'clock found us in a private car hurrying farther and farther to South Florida. At twelve o'clock we reached Maitland, and went

to see an orange grove belonging to Mr. Law-
rence. We were very much pleased, but the
day was hot and dusty and we were tired We
took carriages at Maitland and drove to a little
station three miles farther on, where we met
our car again. At one o'clock we reached
Kissimee, and were hungry and ready for our
lunch, so we hurried over a hot, bare field to
the steamer " Gertrude," which was to carry
the gentlemen to Fort Gardner for several
days' fishing. In the saloon there was a nice
lunch ready for us. As the President stepped
on board, a gentleman of about sixty years
came to him and introduced himself as Sir
Philip Clarke, and begged to be allowed to
join the fishing party. Of course there was no
way of refusing him, and although he was intensely disagreeable, we managed to enjoy our
lunch to the fullest extent. Kissimee City is
filled with negroes of the darkest type. There
are a few badly built houses and one inn. The
people are very ignorant, and seemed surprised
at finding the President a civilized human being. This town is the furtherst south in
Florida accessible by rail. After lunch, Mrs.
Mercer, Hattie, Reginald Fry and I boarded
the train again for Sanford, leaving the gentlemen to fish for a few days on the lakes. Be-
tween Kissimee and Sanford there is an ice
factory, and as neither Hattie nor I had seen

one, we had the train stopped and went through it. We reached Sanford about seven o'clock, and went directly to the hotel for our dinner, after which delightful repast we went out to make a few purchases, then went to our parlor and sat there until bed time.

Tuesday, April 10.— We had breakfast about nine o'clock, as Reggie Fry expected to go home at eleven, but after waiting at the wharf for an hour we found that the steamer was very late, so he decided to stay until the next morning. Hattie and I went out to buy material to make ourselves waists to wear in the evenings. We bought large hats the evening before. Hattie trimmed hers with blue ribbon, and I mine with white mull. We bought some lovely light blue nun's veiling for our waists and hurried home to make them so as to finish them before the President and party returned A dressmaker cut them for us, and then we sewed steadily until five o'clock, when Mr. Trafford came for us to take a drive. We came home about seven and after dinner Mr. Trafford and his better half made us quite a long visit, and when eleven o'clock came we were glad to get to our rooms, not a bit afraid, though we were the sole occupants of the hotel, with the exception of the servants at the other end

Wednesday, April 11.--We all went to the

boat with Reggie at ten o'clock, and on our return to the hotel found a telegram from the President saying that they would all be back in time for dinner. Of course we finished our waists and worked hard to do so. When the train came puffing into Sanford at eight o'clock, we all were on the porch waiting in eager expectation. Hattie and I went away into one end of the piazza, and left Mrs. Mercer to receive the party. After the usual "how do you do?" had been said, we heard the President say: "Nancy, where are the girls?" And nobody knows how glad we were to come from our hiding places and show ourselves. We went to dinner about ten o'clock, and it was indeed " the merriest meal of all " The gentlemen told all about the Indians, and what grand times they had had fishing. We were at dinner until nearly twelve o'clock, then went to our rooms, each ready for a good night's rest.

Thursday morning found us ready and hungry for breakfast about eleven o'clock, and after that delightful repast we sat around upon the piazza, when Mrs Mercer, Hattie, President Arthur and Secretary Chandler went for a drive. I went to my room expecting to spend the rest of the afternoon reading ; but before long I heard a tap at my door, and Mr. Miller and Mr. Phillips calling out : " Hurry,

and come for a walk with us." It took me a
very short time to make my toilet, and presently we three were plodding through Sanford
having a jolly time. Mr Miller bought Hattie and I each a very pretty bird, and Mrs.
Mercer a white curlew's wing We went to a
dry goods store, and he bought some blue rib
bon for Hattie and I to wear with our blue
waists, also some exquisite Irish point lace for
my sleeves. When we reached the hotel we
sat some time on the piazza, and when they
returned from their drive, the President asked
me if I would not take a drive with him, which
invitation I accepted We came home ready
for our dinners after a lively time, and were
not too tired afterwards for the President,
Hattie and Mrs Mercer to walk until twelve on
the lower piazza, and Secretary Chandler and
I to take the halls and upper porch. Mr. Miller retired early, feeling unwell, and Secretary
Chandler, Mr. Phillips and I had quite a talk
after we had finished walking. About one we
said " good-night," and I went to my room
to wait for Hattie and Mrs. Mercer. When
they came we talked until the "wee sma'
hours." .

Friday morning found every one of the
party sick; Mrs. Mercer and the President
feeling better, but all of us the worse for the
dinner the evening before. We kept our

rooms until about two o'clock, when Aleck came to the door and said : " Mrs. Mercer, please be ready to leave on the DeBarry at four o'clock." So, at that time precisely, we were on the steamer, about to look our last on dear old Sanford, where we had had such a glorious time. The evening was lovely, so we sat on deck until tea-time. After tea we came up again, and in spite of the lovely moon and pleasant company, Hattie and I tried to sleep, but in vain. About ten o'clock I started to bed, but when I went to tell President Arthur " good-night," he asked me to sit and talk to him for a while, which I willingly did. When I next decided to go, Mr. Miller insisted upon taking me to my state room door, but when we got there we concluded to sit on the other deck for a while. He sent down for some lunch, and we sat there until Mr. Phillips came and told me that Hattie was waiting for me in our state-room.

Saturday morning we had only time to eat our breakfast before landing at Tocoi, where we waited for the train that was to carry us to St. Augustine. In about half an hour we were on our third railroad trip in Florida Mr. Miller amused us with funny jokes and songs until we reached the oldest town in the United States. St. Augustine is decidedly the nicest place in Florida. It has three fine hotels, the

"Magnolia," "St. Augustine" and "Florida House" The old Market House Square and Cathedral, with Fort Marion, are the best known places of interest. The streets are narrow, and one, Treasury street, is only seven feet wide. The sea wall is a great curiosity. It was built in 1835, and is three feet wide on top, and is ten feet above high water mark. Every person visiting St. Augustine walks here. The view from the wall is magnificent. The United States barracks is the oldest place there. The monument on the plaza erected to "the soldiers of St. Augustine who died for the South," is very interesting to us. The inscription is

OUR DEAD.

Erected by the Ladies' Memorial Association of St. Augustine, Florida, A. D. 1873.
In Memoriam. Our Loved Ones who Gave Their Lives in the Service of the Confederate States.

Opposite St. Augustine is Anastasia island, celebrated for its quantity of coquina, which is not found anywhere else in the United States Most of the houses are built of it, as is also Fort Marion and the old Cathedral. We had to drive about a mile from the station to the city, so one o'clock found us at the Magnolia hotel, while the band played, "See the Conquering Hero Comes." The hotel was quite full, but one corridor was given to the Presidential party. At five o'clock we drove to the barracks and there met nearly every person in St. Augustine. It was the evening of the review, and while the band was playing, Lieutenant Hawskins came to me and asked if there was any especial piece of music I would like to hear, and of course I said : "O, yes, 'Maryland, My Maryland.'" I never heard it played so beautifully as it was then. Before going to the review, Mr. Miller and I went around to see the city, and he bought me a lovely palmetto hat, trimmed with pampas grass, an alligator-skin hand-bag, and a beautiful fan of pink curlew. After leaving the barracks, we drove until nearly dinner-time, when Hattie, Mrs. Mercer and I went out to buy a hat for Hattie, and some gloves for me. When we came home dinner was ready, and we went directly to the dining-room. While we were at the table Hattie was taken quite sick and went to her room, Mrs. Mercer following her. In a few moments I went up and sent Mrs. Mercer back to finish her dinner, and I stayed with Hattie the rest of the evening. About eleven o'clock Mrs. Mercer came up with some lovely roses from the President for Hattie and some strawberries for me. After talking some time we retired, with the assurance that Hattie was much better. And so ended our first day in St. Augustine.

Sunday morning, April 15 — We had breakfast about nine o'clock, and afterwards sat on the front porch for a little while. Hattie was not well enough to go to church, so she and I stayed home alone. We went to our parlor and Hattie tried to sleep while I read to her. After lunch, which was about one o'clock, we sat at our windows listening to the darkeys singing in church. At four, Hattie, the President and I went to the old Cathedral for vespers. It is the oldest building in the United States, having been commenced in 1500. The windows are all in the top of the church. After vespers we went back to the hotel, and Hattie, Mrs Mercer and I wrote home. After dinner we all, with the exception of Mr. Miller, went to the darkey church. When church was over we sat on the porch until bed time, and Mr. Phillips and I had quite a nice walk.

Monday morning we decided to go over and see the "Tallapoosa," the steamer which was to carry us back to Savannah. About eleven o'clock, two or three of the officers of the "Tallapoosa," with Hattie and I, drove up town to be weighed. At one o'clock we went to see the steamer. We had to go from the wharf in a steam launch to the ship, as she was anchored out in the bay. We found her to be a beautiful man of war, and were so delighted that we wanted to leave St. Augustine immediately and cruise around the coast. Mr. Phillips, Mrs. Mercer, Hattie, Secretary Chandler, Lieutenant Merry, Commander Kellogg and another officer and I got into a row boat, belonging to the " Tallapoosa," which was manned by six sailors and towed by the steam launch, and went for a ride on the ocean. When we came to the first line of breakers Hattie and Mrs Mercer became afraid, so they decided to send the row boat back, and Secretary Chandler, Lieutenant Merry, Commander Kellogg and I determined to go in the steam launch as far into the ocean as was safe. We had crowds of fun. When we came back to the " Tallapoosa," Hattie and Mrs. Mercer were pale and sea-sick. Every one said that I was a good sailor and would not be sick on our voyage home. On our return to St. Augustine we went for a visit to Fort Marion, which was built by the Spaniards in 1558. It is perfectly wonderful, and the view from the top is grand. There is an old sergeant who sits at the entrance, and he took great pleasure in telling Mrs. Mercer, Mr. Phillips, Hattie, Secretary Chandler, Mr. Miller and I the most awful tales of olden times. After listening to him for some time we left the fort. Hattie and I had a regular romp on the grounds just outside, and then we all went for a walk on the sea wall.

Tuesday, and our last day in Florida! Mrs. Mercer, Hattie, Mr. Phillips and I had breakfast alone, as Mr. Miller and some friends had gone fishing, and President Arthur and Secretary Chandler had not made their appearance. About eleven o'clock Mrs. Mercer, Hattie and I went for a drive with Mrs. Hawskins. Hattie had lost a very valuable piece of jewelry the evening before, and it worried her very much. We thought possibly it might have been found in the Fort, so we drove directly there, but did not see it. After looking there without success, we went to a beautiful orange grove owned by Mrs. Bell. We had a lovely time, marred only by the fact that Hattie was so worried about the loss of the jewel—a badge—as it did not belong to her, but on our return to the hotel we were greeted with the words "the badge is found." It seems that when we were romping, it had dropped off of Hattie's dress, and the old sergeant had picked it up and sent it to the President. That afternoon Hattie, Mr. Phillips, Mr. Miller and I went sailing with Mrs. Hawskins and some of her Spanish friends. We had a delightful sail and the music from the armory was lovely. After dinner, which was at eight o'clock, we sat on the porch until eleven, when we started for the "Tallapoosa." It was a superb night, and as we were about to tow off to the steamer the band played "We sail the ocean blue," amid the cheering of the crowd and the mournful roar of the breakers, and the splash of the water as the boat rocked to and fro. On our way over, the tune changed to " Maryland, my Maryland," and when we reached the steamer the music sounded beautifully. When we were safely on board, President Arthur and Hattie, Mrs. Mercer and Secretary Chandler and Mr. Miller and I went up on deck for a walk before retiring, and to watch the white-crested billows in the moonlight. The last sound we heard from dear old St. Augustine was the very faintest far-away strains of the ever-lovely melody of " Home, Sweet Home," and so we looked our last on the " Land of Flowers " where we had spent so many happy, happy days.

J J. B.

www.ingramcontent.com/pod-product-compliance
Lightning Source LLC
Chambersburg PA
CBHW032144080426
42733CB00008B/1205